DANIELLE PAFUNDA

SPITE

the operating system
brooklyn new york
c. 2020

the operating system print//document

SPITE

ISBN: 978-1-946031-74-7
Library of Congress Control Number: 2019957650
copyright © 2020 by Danielle Pafunda
edited and designed by ELÆ [Lynne DeSilva-Johnson]
with additional typesetting by Janice Lee
is released under a Creative Commons CC-BY-NC-ND (Attribution, Non Commercial,

No Derivatives) License: its reproduction is encouraged for those who otherwise could not afford its purchase in the case of academic, personal, and other creative usage from which no profit will accrue. Complete rules and restrictions are available at: http://creativecommons.org/licenses/by-nc-nd/3.0/

For additional questions regarding reproduction, quotation, or to request a pdf for review contact operator@theoperatingsystem.org

This text was set in All Ages, Minion Pro, Europa, and OCR-A Standard.

Cover art by Elæ using "ses yeux de fougère in Nadja," an anonymous photo montage from 1963, with torn/distressed overlaid typography of the title and author's name, with abstracted tangent lines and three yellow dots, as though hole-punched through.

The Operating System is a member of the **Radical Open Access Collective**, a community of scholar-led, not-for-profit presses, journals and other open access projects. Now consisting of 40 members, we promote a progressive vision for open publishing in the humanities and social sciences.
Learn more at: http://radicaloa.disruptivemedia.org.uk/about/

Books from The Operating System are distributed to the trade by via Ingram, with additional production by Spencer Printing, in Honesdale, PA, in the USA.

Your donation makes our publications, platform and programs possible! We <3 You.
http://www.theoperatingsystem.org/subscribe-join/

the operating system
www.theoperatingsystem.org
brooklyn & worldwide

ONE: MY HEART

9. These bodies leave lit pain that is unsavory heat of which I am one such failed globe
10. An Aries promised to the dirt as are we all are
12. They put a bracket on my wrist a plastic cuff and said read it backward is it you? So it was and it wasn't.
13. There were times I bred for personal gain though I myself a property incapable of allegiance
15. And seemingly forgotten milk
16. Ever so difficult to slip past the night watch in the manic bohemian dream gate castle for property when you are property I am

TWO: THROUGH WHICH HER HEART

19. When you left me in the rutted terrain of our love at the base of the range which I could not cross remaining a denizen of this corrupt land

THREE: HAS PASSED

55. I came to you and didn't love you and then you cried cuz I was dead
57. Immune to these forms of self-flagellation you look for a field of nettles to corrupt with your untimely flesh
59. I come to you adorned in a moss in which barely visible organisms foment and bioluminescently suggest a foolish joy
62. Don't bring me anything when you come to my door I burrow I don't nest
64. HOSPITAL BOOK! HOSPITAL BOOK!
65. Shhhhhhhhh, shhhhhhhh
66. Shhhhhhhhh, shhhhhhhh
70. In bed with your book the news the news just gapes
71. Impatient to be ratified a skin crawls across your rims a wound closes

Do not expect me to provide an exact account of what I have been permitted to experience in this domain. I shall limit myself here to recalling without effort certain things which, apart from any exertions on my part, have occasionally happened to me, things which, reaching me in unsuspected ways, give me the measure of the particular grace and disgrace of which I am the object; I shall discuss these things without pre-established order, and according to the mood of the moment which lets whatever survives survive.

—André Breton, *Nadja*
translated by Richard Howard

0. MY HEART

The essential thing is that I do not suppose there can be much difference for Nadja between the inside of a sanitarium and the outside.

—André Breton, *Nadja*
translated by Richard Howard

THESE BODIES LEAVE LIT PAIN THAT IS UNSAVORY HEAT
OF WHICH I AM ONE SUCH FAILED GLOBE

I can't take you with me.
The belief that every day must include pain.

The belief that every day must include pain.

The belief that every day must include pain.
I can't take you with me, over there, I can't /
dishonest / belief. But I do. Am I a mother

who loves your mewling / mouthing / creep
into bed and put your hands somewhere
unplayable. What bodies you've seen
thru gauze stuffing, gluey
white bread / body knowing its name
is just skin / not pain as though / everyday
I cannot take you with me. This belief / pain.

AN ARIES PROMISED TO THE DIRT AS ARE WE ALL

Who can do anything now, brides
as we are, impossible brides of
plastic time. It was said / this belief

that every day include pain.

Punching in a sitting-down
position / the moon / between

the well-organized god of war
and her mother, a loose rack
of damaged goods

liquid, covered and thick /
a bird's mouth cannot / feel heat
but can swell. It has a tongue

that every day must include pain.

What's missing? The stars,
the royal we of a virus
issuing new instructions
to old proteins, a candle
in its guttering / gutter / a cave
of roses issuing scent
and camphor ants and a path

that runs down the spine, a river
of substance P / pain. / wait.

Every day must include you, marrow referent,
and every day must include the belief

I can walk to the dump.
I can fit in there.
Travesty reek of strangers' lives

more honey / in which I /
landfill secret slosh debris.
I cannot contain the belief we extract,
tubular, from the earth / inter waste / wait

THEY PUT A BRACKET ON MY WRIST A PLASTIC CUFF AND SAID READ IT
BACKWARD IS IT YOU? SO IT WAS AND IT WASN'T.

How could I know / I was
the other woman and took form

in cyanotic

in cyanotic relationship to ambition, carbon,

the

the primary her / other cyanotic her,
scale monstrous / an ocean of hate,
a hinge unscrewed or screwed

wrong. I was death's other option / paste

I mean to say: I was frothing to death.
I was yellow sap a step back from
the dx / wrist stropping snuff tuff
films of a history in which we trade
for a gummy spread / a life: two deaths,
four deaths, you know how farthers go.

Everyone / I got in the way because I was
hospital! clumsy! And I had lost some blood--

THERE WERE TIMES I BRED FOR PERSONAL GAIN THOUGH
I MYSELF A PROPERTY INCAPABLE OF ALLEGIANCE

This isn't a mother's book. What once
was the high-rent white commune
in my back degrades / and begins /

Remember the time I gave.

I gave birth to a pepper-wing baby
a persistent beat singeing first the gates
and then the gloves and then my breast

blah blah blah. The belief that
everyday must include pain but some
besotted in their small study /

her back / *their* back / guilt

to you. Cold noise delivery. Remember.
Okay thanks. Okay thank you the baby

who spurred / back to / down / to
understand / they, the baby, did this

to take stronghold of me / longer
than leash or yoke or deed,
umbilical *chord*

Make an exit by dripping honey
down the ants' wall. By crossing
species, that radar resistant species

tunneling

with the spoon
from which / milk, camphor / your mother

an exit wound
that doesn't try
to be

pain or everyday or pain

these sailors / have no secrets / nor cells
from which / it's only always water,

daughter.

AND SEEMINGLY FORGOTTEN MILK

Her gets filled with joy as she chew
thru the waxy cap on her cell. Nun,
nectar sister stupefied then loosed

on a field of sting and feed. Her,
simple sign in any garret / wicking
out the window, down smoking
unfiltered from the view or else

a thickness like shower curtain
touch you before her. Her name

changed.

Her name taking on a multidimensional
haunt / when a dream is all about her

it wets the mattress, it weeps the pillow
it dawns dew-soaked then spit / spite.

It's a sort of wave, milk soured in a /
seemingly forgotten / milk / this

belief.

EVER SO DIFFICULT TO SLIP PAST THE NIGHT WATCH IN THE MANIC BOHEMIAN DREAM GATE CASTLE FOR PROPERTY WHEN YOU ARE PROPERTY I AM

It is easy to be nice to someone who isn't me,
anyone / who isn't me. Possum-tooth moon
cutting in line to heap syrups into that pure
pure white cask / bored red spout.

It is easy to be nice to an empty cross
crossroads all four of its devils out

sick

in which it is easy to mistake blood for affection
plenty fleshy skirts and manes. This isn't /
for a very long time unless an accident befell me /

lasting.

I have outlasted the slush, the septic
the shunt that / curls like possum
that person known as *Nadja*

this hyena won't be choked out

    so

easy

II.
THROUGH WHICH HER HEART

Here is the banal expression of my desire, already formulated, not to be in the presence of Nadja, such as she has become [...]

—André Breton, *Communicating Vessels*
translated by Ann Caws & Geoffrey T. Harris

WHEN YOU LEFT ME IN THE RUTTED TERRAIN OF OUR LOVE
AT THE BASE OF THE RANGE WHICH I COULD NOT CROSS
REMAINING A DENIZEN OF THIS CORRUPT LAND

How have I fallen into this hole? Why have I fallen into this hole? Were this hole avoidable, would I have avoided it? If this hole were not bedecked with dried roses and furs, would I have avoided it? Were this hole not located directly in front of my face whichever direction I turn, would I have avoided it? If this hole had fewer magnetic pulses taking place in concentric circles rippling up into my face descending down my body in a slick tube of interference, would I have walked in an impossible direction away from this hole? If this hole weren't serving quite so much whiskey. If this hole didn't show up on my birthday. If this hole didn't shudder and produce books about holes. If I weren't full of holes myself. If I didn't look into the hole like it were a mirror telling me un-hole-some things. If I weren't so clumsy. If this hole didn't appear in traffic just before a bus were to flatten me but down the hole I drop. Were this hole not full of trace evidence. Were no one in this hole before me. Were it possible to be a gracious loving expansive human being outside of a hole. Were it not the sort of day when the wind can shift suddenly. Were the gray sky more than confirmation that the earth exists in a massive hole. Were the hole taking its time still. Had I noticed the hole sitting next to me, so quietly, so many years ago. Had I not previously been a denizen of holes. Were I not a citizen of the hole. If the hole were not the thing that best suits my complexion. Were I not headed straight for the hole when I received the phone call and the signal died and into the hole I tumbled. How have I fallen in this hole? Is this a particular hole? Were there other holes? Is there a place where I could've walked unimpeded for several centuries, with a peacock's feather laced into my habits? Was there once a leash that led to nothing other than my affection and around a rectangular pond we strolled in such brocades as are assembled by people? No. There was just a hole. Hello in here.

I take your books to a city that's being burned by its own inhabitants. *We can't live with ourselves,* they're shouting. I throw your books into the flames. I stand at the base of a collapsing hospital and watch its gurneys roll out in slow motion. Later, I will strap you to a gurney and roll you slowly through the streets of a city whose inhabitants have agreed to live with each other in silent loathing. Eventually even their loathing atrophies. They nod to each other. They nod to me as I roll your gurney down the street, slowing traffic. You're breathing, so let me whisper in your birthmark-studded ear, *this is only practice for your funeral procession.*

Having burned the cord and then some and witnessed a punched-through hole and rinsed the ink again and again from the thick cloth. Having registered deep in my clutch a tremble in an hour past-due and swallowed. Having failed to anticipate the queue. Having stepped into traffic and lost the contents of my face. Having strode partway down the hall. Having completed a sequence of exchanges, recognized a diptych, made an unfortunately nonchalant gesture, decided against the body, held forth. Having given up and given them each word cradled in the spoon's bulb. Having marked and marked and marked again, or occupied a series of categories, some of which did not apply. Having not found a way out of the building without touching its handles. Having ratcheted up to full height. Having requested nicer tones from the beasts of the wood. A pill, which brings me a sense of wellbeing no matter its chemical route. The swallowing. The registering. The frequency with which the day reset and reset again.

It just got so quiet in here. I check my vectors compulsively, reflexively, though I know you've got nothing left to jam into my pneumatic tubes. Traumatic tubes. My boob tube, my tied tube, the tube through which I huff gasoline fumes, the tubes descending from my brain, down which memory slides to gut to gunt to grunt to grain. In me bursts a field of regret, regression, a sharp-grassed, broad-leafed, tick-ridden field. Damp with spit bugs, their frothy suits soaking my jeans. Oh, this is a memory, then. Where I hid in the hayfield under strangesky and hoped it would never end. You see? There are things other than you I hoped and hoped and hoped and hopped up on hope would never end.

I have gone batty with your lack of time for me. I strap the alarm clock to the wall clock to my phone with its ultra-legible display to some watches broken or not, and toss these all in a bucket of wash water and haul this bucket to the backyard to freeze. With electrical tape, I redact the clock on the stove, in the car's dash, on the microwave, the corner of the computer screen, I redact. Where the bells of the university and churches toll, I wrap cotton scarves. Around my head and the heads of the statues, and we can still hear these bells of course I'm not so foolish, it's a gesture, an emblematic refusal to chime.

Having gotten sick on fumes. Having forgotten how to put a block of dry ice in the chest. Having handled the ice bare-handed, handled the ice bare-chested, put the ice in place of the wrong organ, used the ice to cool an organ I no longer wanted. Having mixed the ice with the wrong kind of liquid. Having spilled all down my front. Having stood at the bottom of the stairs, the blank stair the nothing stair under which is lodged every dream of heaven when you're lying on your back and every absence when you're lying on your front. Having feared for myself and curled over like a bleak pebble. Having feared for my selves and wound them up with chain link, my selves running roughshod over the yard, my selves all scrapped in a heap with rusted sawed-off limbs. Having misunderstood the structure of time and how it meant to proceed from here on out. Having thought I could survive speaking aloud and indeed I could but not the words I spoke. Having imagined myself a cool, hoofed animal treading the plain sufficient in her food and water. Having known I would experience swifter degeneration, but not having predicted which muscle would shrug first. Having never before realized how many fine muscles fan out about the act of reading. Having spit on the floor even though I would have to scrub the floor. Spite. Having spit my heart's strange weeds all specked with phosphorescent mites. Answer when I call and answer it again and then when I call, answer, and put me at ease.

Oh storm-damaged sarcophagus of self upended into the day, cracking open to leak its leathered form and grubby ribbons. The yellower self on the run from go. Oh one of two nights that I sleep. *Got it!* You've texted. *I'm busy, but I'll write later!* I do things I haven't before done. I watch porn and take some comfort in its subgenre small tits. I read *The Knotted Subject,* a book that repurposes hysteria, and so is like things I've done before but I haven't read this volume. I underline neatly the phrase it *persistently wanders, as a foreign body, through the psychic and somatic systems.* I hear *psychic* as sidekick. As sidecar. I spell it *sychic* transcribing. The sibilance of loss. Christa calls, and in the presence of that exterior bell, this becomes true. I want to talk to her, but freeze before whisking my finger over the screen. My mother friends me on Facebook, and my gorge rises. I have a gorge, it occurs to me. A throat, a narrow valley, a channel through the wizened self. A hollow column between one swinging gate and the other, my ribcage. A tube that runs behind the heart, or is it before? I map it with coffee, I map it in my mind, thinking it sleek, then thinking it no studded with harm and waste. I can feel miraculous wares drop through the snaking hate of me. I change your name in my phone to *Enough.* I'm imperious and starving and like The Blob I grow larger on each disappointment, though it occurs to me that the blob ate teenagers, disappointment on legs. Later I change it to *Never Mind.*

I fill your face with lawn darts and roll you in hot coals and fiberglass. I take a ½ inch diamond bit and drill a hole in each of your ribs and thread them with aircraft cable. I remove your eyeballs and replace them with rocks too large for the sockets so that your cheekbones fracture. On the back of the rocks, I've smeared industrial strength putty, but I still need to lash them to your crushed face when you run from the dogs at night. You're barefoot. Stones and glass kick up, blood runs down your shins, your calves. You sniff for the river, you run toward the river. You're an ancient ballsack of underworld fame. You try living in a ditch, but you aren't cool enough to get in. You live in a pipe. Mildew, mold, love potion number 24 cologne. You eat hot dogs for breakfast and brew your coffee with the water in which the hot dogs were cooked. You bed down in a nest of eyelashes, typewriter ribbons, disposed safety razors. You get plowed. I plant portulaca in each of your orifices, weeding and watering diligently all summer long. I have a rusty soil scoop my brother swiped from the garage in 1983. He used it to kill squirrels, birds, frogs. I use it on you, now. You keep swallowing mouthful after mouthful of my rust-flecked soil. Worms won't live in you, but they slum there for kicks. I catch you licking the tines of a rake from which dangle dead leaves, used condoms, and loose clumps of earth. I feed you cigars for snack time and play YouTube videos of middle-class couples smearing themselves in yogurt and honey. I've seen you wave your pun-vessel at passers-by on the busiest street corner in the neighborhood. You carry an unweaned kitten whom you won't let drink her mama's milk until you've had your fill. It's embarrassing to be caught in the range of your pheromones, a special mix of bandage and spittle. You grow mushrooms in a wet paper sack to cover the smell of your molting ideas.

I feel your funeral. I describe for you the dress I've purchased to wear to your funeral. I describe to you the run I'll get in my stocking as I lean over the grave's raw edge.

Your teeth are still nicely ridged, so when they shatter on the pavement where the dogs pin you down, I will collect them. I will rinse those fragments and pat them dry with a special kind of muslin cloth. Then I will weave a nest from my own fine, dark strands saved from the bath, the pillow. I'll stiffen this nest with lacquer, and nestle the broken teeth inside, and when they look too lonesome these baby birds, I will steal into your room at night with a dropper full of anesthesia and when you are thoroughly unconscious beyond dream, I'll pluck out a nice fat eye tooth, a robust mama to set in her nest, etc.

Eat pavement. Every house I've ever built, I've had to leave in a liminal state. I've had to exist in limbo, bag in hand, becoming bag, I am a bag. I sag, I fill and spill over, my seams strained. Oh, also, I'm a bag lady. A kind of lady with bags, the bags under my eyes, and I bag you in field and you say, *fuck, what now?* What now? What next? Whatever shall we do? Nothing, sweet beet. I tie a leather cord round the maw of the bag, and into the bed you go. The pickup's bed. Down a rutted road. Down toward the pond, where there are so many fire ant mounds. Past the barn that apes the barns that once were, its red steel impression. I'm gonna drop you off. I'm gonna let you down. Easy. But you ought to be out there eating pavement. You ought to do that for awhile, considering your role in all of this and wondering to yourself *how might I improve my performance in the future*. Which future doesn't exist, but baggage.

I live in the destroyed section of town known as your face. Gunshots go off in your face. Your face eats the pavement and pavement scrubs your face. I squeeze tighter the wire lining of my bra hoping to keep it from riding up my small breasts. My breasts in your face appear, in their cheerful stance and material deficit, hopeless. In your face, I prepare a spare meal and then sicken it into the toilet. The rent on your face is high, there go my pennies into your gob, there goes all my savings into your cracked mug, there goes my retirement, my futures, my stocks and bonds. It's bondage. I'm lashed to your face. I lash against your face. When your restitched tongue reluctantly licks me, I squirm. With something. Rather unlike pleasure. I'm restricted. There are no pets or children allowed. There is no blowing smoke or throwing drinks or spitting in your face. The security deposit was a cringe. I relearn the act of navigating public space in the wake of your face. I find that we do not allow for the unusually embodied in the greater expanse of public space I tread, I tread your face.I'm not going to say I have a perfect record, but I have a record I'm proud of.

I can't stand my life without you. I can't stand my face without you. I can't stand here without you without shivering so hard I bite my tongue, repeatedly, blood pools at the back of my teeth. Blood sets on my bottom lip. I gave you nothing except access. Wasn't that enough?

Last night you decided you needed some space.
You moved to the other side of the island,
but the island is small and I can see you
build your shelter from here. You won't
look at me. You're hauling fronds and vines,
stopping to squeeze clean water from a rag
into your mouth. So I climb down from the rock
where we lay our clothes to dry and burn fires
all night in the SOS-shape. I calmly apply
powdered oyster shells to my eyelids and stain
my lips with crushed berries. Maybe poisonous.
Not for you, sitting with your back to me
on the far side of the island, which has the best view
of sunset. I hold a shard of mirror and paint my face
for myself. For the interview I later conduct with myself.

> Q: What was it like when he left?
> A: It was hard. I could still see him. I slept alone
> in our gritty bed, and continued to weave
> sea grass mats for two. When he cut his foot
> on a jagged rock near shore, I watched him
> hobble and bleed. I watched him expertly
> bandage it with seaweed.
> Q: What happened to your hair?
> A: It fell out.
> Q: What happened to your arms?
> A: At first the lacerations were accidental.
> Then we saw a pattern and connected them.
> This was before he left.
> Q: Which of you was the first to cry out
> when sand fleas invaded your bed?
> A: I was.
> Q: Which of you was the first to imagine
> you saw a ship on the water?
> A: He was.
> Q: Which of you is more tired of dreary
> afternoons, huddled under palm fronds
> scratching poems into bark?

A: *That's a manifesto you're holding.*
Q: Forgive me. Indeed it is. Let's move on.
Which of you is the funny one?
A: *I am.*
Q: That must be very difficult.
A: *It is.*

Q: What happens when he puts his cock in you?
A: *Someone goes hungry.*
Q: What happens when he puts his cock in you?
A: *It plunges into a wasps' nest.*
Q: What happens when he puts his cock in you?
A: *I drunk-dial.*
Q: What happens when he puts his cock in you?
A: *Nobody move.*
Q: What happens when he puts his cock in you?
A: *Twelve lords a'leaping.*
Q: What happens when he puts his cock in you?
A: *I lay an egg.*
Q: What happens when he puts his cock in you?
A: *He fills my ring.*
Q: What happens when he puts his cock in you?
A: *I douse the flares in ocean water.*
Q: What happens when he puts his cock in you?
A: *I set the ocean on fire.*
Q: What happens when he puts his cock in you?
A: *I plunge a coral stake deep in my h-art.*
Q: What happens when he puts his cock in you?
A: *Something foolish.*

Q: Tell me about your lover?
A: *My lover is five-pronged. My lover has
metal stars embedded in his back, one for
each time he did his job. He doesn't take
any pills or any advice. His lips are full
and glumly set so that one must kiss them
cover them in public with her hand
or her scarf, quickly turn him 'round
so that the crowd won't see
sob themselves, to their knees, wretched—*

Q: The public?
A: I'm talking about the past.
Q: What is your lover like, now, on the island?
A: He's the same. Except his mouth
is even sadder, and I can't see into his eyes
because the angle of the sun, it's always behind him.
His skin runs like a promise against another skin
in the night and in the day it washes up like a shell.
The reeds in his throat twine and expand,
and moonlight huddles in his nail beds.
He warms the bed like a brick from the fire,
then runs his cool hand down my bare back.
Q: Does he really?
A: Yes. He has two hearts. One for everyday use
and one for me. He is of one mind, which is why
he moved to the other end of the island.
There are no pebbles on his makeshift sill.
He marks the days on a tree trunk deep in the forest.
He receives a kiss with much good grace, and fucks
me closer to death. His cock is forged and flecked bronze
from its time as a monument to optimism. It fits
the ring in the center of my skepticism, and never
misses a beat.
Q: Is there anything else?
A: His fangs, his tail, his hooves, his horns.
His nostrils flared, his foot on my thigh. His
reason, his faith, his fate, his fear. His clutches,
his traps, his furs, his flowers. His children
all nestled, his webs, his nests. His tools,
his travails, his hand cupping my tail, his loss,
his purse, his pennybox, his nicklenip, his dimestore,
his quarterhorse, his half-penny will do. His thighs
beneath me when I'm astride, his face in my neck.
His fancy dress, his black tie, his Romeo, his plans
for later, his wristwatch, his tempest cup, his sun-
scarred shoulders spread out under constellations
I don't recognize or never knew. His failure.
His freedom. His scent that I lap from his face,
the salt that I lick from him, his stomach that I rest,

his brow that I return to, his chest in which I bury
a little bomb to go off repeatedly, but the fucker simply
won't kill us.
Q: Is that an admission?
A: No.
Q: Do you love him very much?
A: I have no one left to be who doesn't love him so.
Q: What did he take when he left?
A: He took a quill, a stack of parchment bark, one of the snails
we keep as pets, some hibiscus flowers, a fishing spear,
cooking salt, a piece of quartz we use to ward off bad dreams,
my thumbprint in squid's ink on a well-rounded stone,
the rest of the morning's coffee, two red feathers, his clothes,
his name, that way of sighing through his nose, his heavy hand
when he's done with a cup, his darkened lids
at the end of the night, his snaps and hoots and whistled tunes,
his laugh, my laugh, the laugh the parrots mimic, the parrots
whisper now, and what they say is tickle, tickle on your knee,
if you laugh then you don't love me!

Once when we were thrown overboard tied round the waist in a rickety pine box and the box began to fill quickly with water while you searched for a way out I couldn't stop saying *you complete me*. And *Heaven is a place on earth*. And *I can see forever in your eyes*. Even as salt water stung my lips, I molted. Peonies burst live, heavy from my tongue. I was covered in warm sugar wax. When you tried to cover my mouth, your hand stuck in the pitch I was dribbling. You loved me then, gruesome little parrot, record-scratch siren, sticky dying insta-eyed. We had no axes, no matches, no knives. No crowbars, no flashlights, no clever ideas. Until the waves themselves got tired of us, and spent our grave against some rocks.

My lover who got free of me. My lover who got free of me to joy, my lover who got free of me to plainer skies my lover who held a crossbow to his throat as he backed out the door, my lover who called me no thanks my lover who was in it for the money my lover who was unwell and lay his head down on the tracks, my lover who lay down his shield, my lover who waited quietly braced between beams and then dropped from the ceiling onto the nurse's back my lover's nurse, my lover's friend, my lover's shirt stuffed behind the radiator that dripped and dripped and the floor rot through I saw the beams beneath. Deep into the earth the lovers braced then dropped, dropped, dropped, we were all more wolves than rats, rats than worms, worms than molten, and molten depth. The belief that everyday. I was always the adulterous bride of pain.

Having attempted and attempted again to achieve balance where balance was vulgar. Having failed again to draw a conclusion. Having ridden from the camp to the homestead and back several times. Having noticed a strange sensation that turned out to be my heart stuffed full of prawns and tried to remove these prawns from my heart only to discover millipedes. Having previously lived in a mansion full of millipedes. Having had to wait patiently as millipedes arrived with snapshots from the past. Having recognized the multidirectional bodies of transparent scribes. Having ignored the cat when she dragged, rather than one of those harbingers from under the carpet, a paper heart from the mantel and dropped it at my feet. Having filled up on prawns so that the prawns in my heart might know what was coming for them. Having found myself replete with squirming life. Having held a warm sack of oats. Having sat still long enough to warm my back against the fire. Having set the fire in a metal can at the edge of the property. Having looked into the can as I dropped each snapshot, or letter, whatever, I had a fistful of ephemera somehow connected to me in name. Having then escaped into the city where I wrote my name in the stalls of dives and on the sidewalks in ash and in the harbor I etched my name into the side of a great many shipping containers. Having procured a number not for a telephone but for a place in line getting slugged in the gut. Having willingly gone into the slug. Having opened my mouth for the slug and swallowed. Having taken it with grace. With grace. Like someone who believed there were grace.

I get very nervous about all the babies you're trying to make. You're trying to make a lot of babies with a woman your parents know. She is very fair skinned and very fair eyed and very fair. You put your penis in her repeatedly. You coat your penis in a protein solution that nourishes and aids motility. You have a scab on your finger and it rubs roughly against her fair labia when you adjust to the proper angle. Her bottom is propped up on a pillow. You put your penis in and will it to make a baby. You have made six babies with four women. Two of the babies live with two of the mothers in the gutter out front, and they spit wads of bread at you when you leave for work in the morning. They spit coffee at you and yell *have a good day at the office, Daddy!* They spit the evening paper at you when you return home. They spit fedoras and sheepskin slippers and lit pipes. They spit the past, but not your past. Two of your other babies have cut up your past and sold it via ads on Craigslist. Their mothers have gotten rich off the stock market and don't care what the babies do for money. You live with the last two babies. The fair woman is their mother, and the babies are young enough to call her Mama. They look just alike, and though they aren't twins, you can't remember which one is older. They're girls. She calls them both Bunny. They lie at the foot of the bed while you try to make yet another baby. You're hoping for a one that looks like you. For one that doesn't side with its mother.

Having read the graffiti on the side of the water tanks. Having climbed into a partially deconstructed forklift being careful to step over a loosely coiled chain with a hook at the end the size of my face. Having dropped my cell phone in the reservoir. Having deleted your number a long time back. Having replaced your number with the decade in which I knew you. Having replaced your number with the number of times I found myself face-down on a strange carpet, sticky beside you. Having lit on fire your number. Having known your number was wrong in the first place. Having found thick stalks of milky grass growing up through the gear shaft. Having fit my bare foot into the rough v of your fingers, slid in and out of your line of sight one-hundred-thousand times, given you all the keys to all my cars, torn my skirt on your old-fashioned latches, eaten whatever we could find in the gaping hole of your kitchen at four am in a bad part of town solely bad because we were in it. Your voice is like that of an angel's who's smoking and dead and otherwise involved.

The whole summer came and went, I wasn't sure if you loved me. Everything was gray. That is, the storm rolled in each afternoon. I wanted to make babies, too, but I was alone, wasn't I? I fashioned some babies out of cornhusks and mud, old-fashioned babies. I stitched some babies onto poster board. I drew babies in the dirt with a stick and these babies held sticks with which to draw babies of their own. When the hail storm crushed the portulaca, I glued the torn petals to popsicle sticks, jaunty little verbena hats.

Having realized I am much younger than other hags. Having stitched a hagfish-skin jumpsuit. Having gone semi-nude into the world with all the marks of a breeder.

I remove your glasses, place them in the cup holder, and then jam a pressure gauge in your eye. PSI fail. With epoxy, I secure your seatbelt forever. I cram your fists into an early twentieth-century vintage fur muff, and hook a yoke about your neck. Through its metal eyes, I thread bungee cords, and loop these through the steering wheel. You're prepared. There's a year's worth of spilled fries on the floor of the backseat, and these I feed you, some clumped together around a hoarfrost penny, others one by one, a little gravel, ladybug shells, acrylic fibers. In the glovebox, I've stored all your letters. Not letters to me. I've been collecting your letters. Off hard drives. From email accounts I hack into. I don't hack into them. I pay my brother to hack into them. He brings me your letters. You sign your messages with *so much love*. It's as though you actually feel this love for a great number of people. As though you can't sleep at night if you haven't told them. Sometimes you spell it *luv* as though to downplay the sick, spidery spread in your chest, but just poorly enough that your sincere deep affection shines through. There are so many letters. When the glovebox fills, I put them in the trunk. Your receipts, receipts that remind me of you, a list of groceries I suspect you have purchased. Where is all this going? I lift the brake. I align the wheels. I clock my knee on the steering column's unforgiving plastic sheath. I tumble over you out the door, and roll, and roll. And listen. And splash. And there you are with your tongue cut out and knives in your legs and forever turned to froth that can't say goodbye and relies on the few moments of real goodness in children to keep its rhythm awash against the only rock you recognize. For miles around. What dirty prince led you to this? What dirty crown swayed above his head while you made your rich choices?

In your absence I stop taking my pills. Instead, I crush them, all kinds, and dissolve them in the coffee urn in your mailroom. Soon, your entire department is spinning. People run hot, people put their hands through the thin panes of glass in the building's old windows, people say they *didn't see it coming*. When you pass out in the men's room, leaning over the sink, soaking your shirtsleeves as you pitch forward, then crumpling onto the tile so perfectly I stop to take a picture and run it through one of the app's aesthetisizing filters. Then I straighten you out. I pull your shirt down where it's come untucked. I arrange your arms by your sides. I place a thin sheet over you, head to toe. I place a card on the tile beside you. It says your name, your birthdate, today's date. It says: *Causes: UNKNOWN.* I slip down the back staircase, where I find two neatly-suited women locked in a deep tongue kiss, and feel warm. I have done good in the world. Later, when your colleagues find you, they will panic. In a maelstrom of serotonin, norepinephrine, and dopamine, on a weird mix of uppers and downers, with a blast of antihistamines and steroids, they'll assume they've become the morgue. They'll assume a killer's on the loose. They'll assume the worst of you. They'll rifle through your desk looking for your mother's phone number, the numbers of your children's mothers. They won't be able to crack the passcode on your phone. They'll forget how to use phones. They'll text each other puking-skull-emoji panic. They'll turn out the bathroom lights out of respect, and someone will light a contraband candle. Sandalwood. Someone will leave the fifty dollars he lost to you in a poker game two months ago in your coat pocket. Someone will suggest everyone have a cup of coffee in the conference room, which will start the whole cycle over again.

Come back when you want something I have. Put on your clean pants and your good shirt and your jacket with the brass buttons and come to my door when you want something that's already here. Run into the river that's running with broken glass and bodies and chemical debris and the plastic beaks of industry. Stand there when you want something I have and raise your arms above your head and wave them. When you want something I have, send me a text. Text me a picture of your mouth with your lips dried out and your tongue coated white and your teeth about to close around a flash drive. Give me a list of dogs. Give me a list of trashcans. Give me a list of discarded sandwich wrappers. Give me a list of dead grandmothers. Give me a list of drowned rats. Give me a list of unnecessary tourniquets and lost maps. Give me a list of desperate sailors. Give me a list of men who failed to find the witch in time. Give me a list of witches whose lights go out. Give me a list of tournament losers. Give me a list of line-waiters their skin crawling with lice. Give me a list of backseaters. Give me a list of the back-burnered. Give me a list of those who want it less than you and maybe I'll give it. Maybe I'll still have something to give.

Well didn't you leave me here? Didn't you leave me here in this field of nettles and prickly pear, all their medicine trilling behind barbs? Didn't you leave me barefoot to pick my way through nest upon nest of ants, acid-laced ants, again weapicine. Call for the wahmbulance! I am too weepy to wade through my own vision. The plains watch me weep and ready their fiddles. Oh Susanna, Clementine, my darling Sunshine. I'd rather be the she who goes. I'd rather hoof it into the sunset until I become just a lyric. But there's the rub. A lyric is a body that lays on the page and light as a feather stiff as a board pierces you through the sweetmeat throat time and time again. It's an instrument that starts you humming and hums back at you, in time, its teeth barred. Let me tell you something, since you're gone and I've no one to speak to but this oddly mossy rock, this flat hard moss that survives on next to no water, let me tell you old mossy pal, that I do not relish having been left alone here in conditions that I did not alone create. *Nor I* would the moss say if it knew any better. Rocks, blue skies, bullshit everyone in town says will heal you.

So I am alone, now. I choke on hair. I cannot drive or chop wood and I certainly cannot rise before dawn, so I begin to slaughter those things that can. I kill a rooster and hack its comb free and it sings. I put a tension rod through an engine block. I choke this axe with hair. You are lucky, for when you drop by, my axe is bound in hair and when hefted halts and weighs above us like a spirit for whom we've no board from which to call. She rides above us like a water witch, a broom gone far too far. Her tears are made of hair and her hair is like that of an entire colony of drowned rats. A dead meat. Her meat is made of hair and kills its way in the slow intestine. Nothing happens quickly anymore. We got to the future and it moved terribly slow around us. Slowly. I was so swift. I outpaced it and returned any number of times until one day I was tired and said *I would like to die now*, but the future could not be reached for at least thirty years. I thought about it some more. It was forty years. It was a lifetime, barring any intervention, it was a whole 'nother lifetime. In it, you were a daguerreotype. The plate had caught your wig and above it the blade with a wig in its gut and a wooden hard-on for going places. Later I was photographed with the same wraith, and my smile that shows slightly pointed canines as though what I cannot outpace is my animal past, which is true, I cannot. Did you know? Did you know me when I was telling you clearly line by line who I was. Did you hear the one about the hour that went by on this very night when I thought I might die but for my fat charges stacked up behind the door? If I open that door, they'll tumble out on me, and my shame over this hour will replay. Did you hear that? It is this hour ticking through the anyweaponsinthehouse. It is the hissing of logic that hits the pan and evaporates on contact the pan is a metaphor I spell it meataphor, I think, that's funny, I think I still think things are funny, this hour is passing moment by moment. You don't surface. I wonder if someone should dive in after you. That would be me. You would worm out of my grasp. I would say: I am drowning. You would say: there is nothing here to get drowned about.

Before dawn, I come to write my name in your yard. To write my name in piss in the snow. I have a thick paper funnel so that I can pee standing up. I have a larger silicone funnel and a jar full of urine to complete the task. It's quiet on your block. Blue-running-pink in the new snow sunrise. Your windows are darkened yet. Sometimes I wish I believed in a merciful entity so that I could cry out *take mercy on me*. I cover as much ground as I can with tights and panties around my thighs, skirt hiked, messy business to some degree, but the steam rises up and I'm like those little boys who have just learned it's possible. To write one's name not as a parochial chore, but gleefully. I survey my work, careful to brush away my footprints but not disturb the little twigs, berries, bits of gravel that have blown across the canvas. Which of your wives lives here, now? I can't recall. Which of your children will spring fresh from her bed, curly hair tumbling over her forehead, a plaintive whelp, it's breakfast time and far too cold on the hardwood floors? I order my clothes, tug down my skirt, my parka falling over it, some comfort to my frosty ass, I'm presentable by the time the first hardcore jogger puffs by. She may be the only one. A man in a fur hat follows with two shivering terriers. I wonder if the fur is real. I wonder what the dogs know, smell. A late delivery of the morning paper. I fold the front page into a sailboat. I fold the next page into a crane. Too easy. I fold hearts and giraffes and anything I remember. I make six-pointed stars, my fingers numb. I drop each one in the snow, to melt there. The paper melting, the water holding steady as though a layer of powder could cover up this blemish. How is my heart doing, anyhow? Has it bled through that paper sack you call your arms? Has it begun to wriggle in your teeth when you open a bit to seek better purchase? Has it gone cold and smooth and clean as a saint? Is it, like me, wrapped in plaster, unashamed on its face? Put it in the attic, love. Make it a bed of rags and burlap. Give it a box with a lid and an ample dose of camphor. A few of your neighbors now, their lights on, one leaves for work and nods at me, unsure, turns back, nods again because I smile, tilt my head, raise my shoulders as though saying, *oh, you know how one must do*. And he smiles, too, before he sets about knocking snow from his car. He claps his gloved hands together. The muffled sound of miles to go. Do I know how much I love you? I don't. You have my heart, my measure. Check her and see. Your light goes on. Check the sheets for stains and your mouth maybe tastes metallic, strange as a flesh penny, the sort a body springs on you so unexpectedly. Who was I when you cupped my chin on an icy morning, on a deserted street that was secretly scheduled for demolition? We were under the wire when you looked down at me, and my skin said yes, and my breath said yes, and there is a hole in the ground where once I said yes. So I wrap the funnels in plastic and along with the last few sheets of newsprint they go neatly back into my bag, a vegan bag, pretty stylish, I didn't dress like a burglar. I reseal the jar, wipe it down, and tuck it in the snow bank a city plow has left at the end of your drive. I'm here to *give*, and *give*, and *give* you anything I have left. My mark and my seal. Any steam from the warmth of my body has long since drifted off, any warmth in my body is, too, drifting off. The tip of my nose has gone noticeably cold. Once a cognitive behavioral therapist told me the tip of the nose is rarely in pain so focus your consciousness there, and I do. Once a dialectical behavioral therapist entreated me to perform the opposite of my urge, which was to perform urge's opposite, so here I am. It's time to leave your yard, but I can't. I'm one of its wayward winter birds plucking nothing from ice for a nothing breakfast. I'm one of its worms deep in the loam waiting for spring that may not come before my death. In the corpse of a snowman, a squirrel gnawed carrot, or less goofy just the number on the mailbox that has come loose, but still the mail finds its right home. Oh, don't worry about me. Oh, I'm fine calling out for a bit of mercy from no one in particular, the sort of mercy a coffee delivers, and anyhow I'm a very rich person in comparison to persons with no beds and no meals. I ought to volunteer my time. If only all my time weren't dedicated to you, hadn't taken up residence in your orbit. I'm out of time because there it is swaying around your body as you haul yourself out of bed and straighten your boxers and spill some grinds and cajole the children, eggs or oatmeal. Can you believe this is what we amount to most days? Any number of times, before I met you, I could not believe it, and yet I performed it with such grace and still do. Excepting this morning, when I stand in your yard, my signature not quite as striking as I'd imagined, but it'll have to do. The planks that prop my chest open, the temporary shunts and silicone valves, the morning birds and rising traffic. Everything hums as it should, now doesn't it? I'll save knocking on your door for another day. I'll save placing something wet and warm in a bag on your doorstep for another day. We're not down to that, quite yet. Not such a thing. In fact, we have a lifetime for this, for I've just signed the deed, and you, unwilling thief, don't give back my heart. Keep it, bed it, fuck it, face it, place it on ice or in a humidor or behind that book on your shelf you can no longer take down. This is my gift to you, nothing but unhinged flesh. Love me, still.

I confess unto. My thoughts have been with men. I have been occupied by men with men and on men have put a thousand hours and dollars and all my reason. It is men that take me full fold into that closet over there and score me baseline. I have relapsed into men. I confess, I have not thought to otherwise work or have supplied anyone anything—other than men I have supplied men with themselves. I have wrapped with tape a sturdy pole to the back of men and set them tall in the yard so that they might consider what they wanted next. I have prone my prone self next to them their prone forms as they leaked tears and said themselves they loathed and hated and those selves would only hurt me and might I sit still or prone stay placed or roll ever so slightly into the narrow sheath between stained comforter and exhausted plaster crackling. I shall. I have not been able to heal. To heel. The marks, the punctuation, the cloud there on my temporal lobe left and temporal lobe right, they are no big deal, they are the marks of men. That is unfair, they are the marks of my relationship to men. I confess, I have been with men. I have been occupied by men they put inside me their separate heat that function of theirs that cock that moves in and against their accord those cocks that say there is something here other than men. I say, lodged up against, clocked into, wound with a key, dramatized by a prick, I say grace and mean it. I confess. What men have asked me to do I have done. I have done it and not done other things. I have on behalf of men considered my own self a luxury no longer able to justify. I have considered my own self a choppable commodity and gone chop chop all day for several weeks at the base of my head. Chop chop. I have thought myself a girl when I am old and have thought myself too old and have said I am too old to be a cutter. Which was true, so everybody laughed. I have explained the ways of men such that everybody laughed, but I confess, I took them seriously. I took men into my bed and under my competent wing and up against the bald spot each bird has on its chest for no other reason one can imagine except for in its death to taxidermy and create a simulacrum of its life far more tranquil than its life for we know, I confess, the life of the birds to be as vexed as any hungry creature. I have eaten worms for men. I have thrown up my worms to nourish men, and I have been a body that grows in it men. What have I done oh lord, my lords, my work, my sisters, my babies most of all, when I have been with men and not with thee?

(a *defense* against the possibility of Nadja's return, whether sane or not, a Nadja who could have read my book about her and have taken offense at it, a *defense* against the involuntary responsibility I might have had in the elaboration of her delirium, and, consequently, in her internment […]).

—André Breton, *Communicating Vessels* translated by Ann Caws & Geoffrey T. Harris

I CAME TO YOU AND DIDN'T LOVE YOU AND THEN YOU CRIED CUZ I WAS DEAD

The return of that person referred to as Nadja
whose return author made / tried / bind
by ending the book / also a fibrous beast
a fibrous breast / banshee /whose many spines
leak off many shelves / do they not / replicate?

The return of that person *sane* or otherwise, author,
the return of that person having aged as people do
yellowing, teeth / smell of bandage, her face /

A mercy the return of that person previously
dissected for her juice. Who was preserved in juice.
Damp and salty / wet ash seeps out the eye

a nightmare is a hole in the membrane
of an otherwise discreet fellow. A nightmare
is to look at the night and see things. A night

the dark, an overripe sky / about to cream its seeds

what does it knock up with? / what happens next

a seed in the throat expands to press vocal chords
so tightly one to another that vibration cannot occur.

Loss of resonance. / A person referred to
the belief that every day must include pain.

The night is cold and greasy. A skin forms where
the night should be. A mare runs, her greasy
milk leaks from her foal and her milk
ferments and her milk becomes a medicine
for your Marxist hardon. Someone rubs it there.

That's you. You're stroking your means.
Because I came to you and did not love you and
I came back to you and loved you not
and I came again, all at a gallop.
You cried cuz I was dead / and then was not.

IMMUNE TO THESE FORMS OF SELF-FLAGELLATION YOU LOOK FOR
A FIELD OF NETTLES TO CORRUPT WITH YOUR UNTIMELY FLESH

This single experimental arc
a series of blots and dashes, red as
the plane's meager cross-continent
does no more than gray your vision.

Come here. / You say. / Slap me
with your hand so cool it stings
and soothes. / Come here. / You

From whose hair / have you woven
this mat / toss

from whose oven taken these
hot coals, the shoals slammed
with a coarse cream, the lover
who bit her tongue and again
she bit her tongue. She said

naught.

Not, come here fuckstick and give yourself
a tight squeeze. You might feel better.
Not lick it. Not stick it. Not suck it.
Not take it from me. Nor give it back.
Not I do not love you, though she no longer
if ever she did, upon finding that where

there were s'posed to be / a you
there was a tremendous nest / fire
ants / acid running down her wrists
where she burst those blisters / half-
sterilized pin from your bygone / half-
punk / a house in which the mattress

never dried out

nor warmed up.

Whose blood. Whose blood spilled
like bluud and not enough. Whose
blue tablet-crusted mouth went numb?
A number we dialed a number we
didn't dial a text sed *what r u doing?*
Who r u gunna b now, mf?

There's not a gutter iced
enough with broken glass and shit
nor a field of nettles fine
enough to create the sort of micro-
aggression your body thinks it longs

the songbirds / know the score /
keep singing / you scored / and scored
to found yourself a score / of lacerations
counted naught. Like every time before.

Have bad dreamz, be the other / thing.

I COME TO YOU ADORNED IN A MOSS IN WHICH BARELY VISIBLE
ORGANISMS FOMENT AND BIOLUMINESCENTLY SUGGEST A FOOLISH JOY

Well perhaps I wanted / to be wanted
like a territory. Entered, ungraspable.
Neither apron / strings nor peninsula
nor anything you could suck / an egg

a turkey-sucking pigeon hole

a pie hole a cram shack a tab
of acid-tongued wave against tundra.
Who's the bear? Gusted white in
the fungal weep but that bear finds
a red snack. That tiger? That tiger

is dead and that tiger is dead and the tiger
with the yawn-maw, the widest yap
of any mammal / goes missing.

Who couldn't enter those jaws? Who
wouldn't? Like the eel, but here on land
in old footage, grainy, melting / my mallet
gives a beat for animal / a beat for the minuscule
chance of recovery. To recover. What has.

Gone missing in me. Gone barely documented
bare in the frame that documents with such ease
with a faint whirr, with our friends searching
the back of the cabinet and coming up

everclear / or / killing each other
in the dry creek bed littering bones
lit up with flesh, lit up with skin with
skings, wings, glitter, fetish, skein

who happened? You never happened to
but upon me. You came here. You cried

lovers' names like *Ohio Arkansas Kansas
City Alabama Baker Down East Back
East North Country High Plains Chicago.*

Do have someone spell you no mother
to visit / a destination.

Knowing all of what I know
and at least half of what you do,
you / who know / just your own
smirk. I'm such a thing?

You can disregard.

Near the sack of fossils
a time machine near
irradiated properties that were
once inside what is inside
inside the fine sheet of muscle
near sheet music nearly done
near wild not near not near.

Not near enough. Not never.
A thrash of lime-laced serum
pours down the gulley / it's a
quarry / it's a ravine / it's a

race.

Not near enough. This is your
weapon blunt and this your
weapon sharp and this your
trauma / opera / option.

It's similar to having a choice,
except that you only have
your own knowledge
on which to rely and when you
explain me, explain us, explain

why you were correct. That every day
must include pain.

DON'T BRING ME ANYTHING WHEN YOU COME
TO MY DOOR I BURROW I DON'T NEST

That every day must include
its clutch / egg-
like seers caught up
by raven/nous. Who knows
how long I'll hang here
like this dreading.
A swell wave of dope / seed
flushes exposed
I piss / through a slit
in my hide
the hide the blind the beard
given / like the finger
meant only for each one
in its arc / wink / stamen
its stale mate

I can't let go of the dishonest belief /
disbelief / the belief that every day.

I believe that every day.

The perfect tremolo of cracked
sidewalk, wet stockings, worn heels
wet plaster, plaster stockings, cast
of an impoverished nothing / that is
futureless sign of history / whose marble

eye

tells you when to leave the city
speaking not your name but your code name

Who turns your chill into business.
You're leaving town and leaving town
and the further you retreat the closer /
death door. The fortune teller gives.

A reading. Take it. Take a story
you can't take away. Take it.

Like a man. In a story.

A small lover a droll lover a lover full
of prawns. A lover whose eyes weep
the fine legs of torched insects, mouth
weeps a ledger, a voice like a ledge
off which you won't leap, but will.

HOSPITAL BOOK! HOSPITAL BOOK!

That person referred to as Nadja disappears
into the hospital you can't / see her / because

you won't

visit her / because / she disappears into security
footage / the nurses keep casual watch / all night
she sleeps vapor sleep or if she does not / they will her.
She can visit any time she likes / from their control
room a nurse / will peel off / fine as a bandage
silken as the history book / a not-now bewitching.

Any time she likes she can be professionally held
emptied of food sex money comfort, receive
a hollow reciprocity within which a real condolence

sounds

so safe to sleep all night a pearlescent eye in the corner
watching the trill of sleepers reflect off the windows
of the medication / the medication always secured
in bottle buoy body / one pill / at a time recorded
her date stamped arm that person referred to /
as Nadja says thank you.

SHHHHHHHHH, SHHHHHHHH

It's late and I have left no one.
Oh Hospital Book!
My life's work has been praised
with injunction to do more, and
more prestigiously, as though /

I weren't now bound / repurposed
to less, in service to / when one

spends too long on men, she loses /
all her girlfriends / such hospital!
gone abroad. She loses the bead

on the finest trail / breadcrumbs are where
the hospital! rat finds her future / mapped
whim of wind and trod. That person

referred to as Nadja in letters, redacted,
that person keen on knowing how this
advice / wishing to comply good patient
with all advisement / but the fail

the white fix

is in the hospital! works.

What a weight invisible friends have her shoulders
do roll them back and cinch the blades till cutting
harvest comes and others wheat does swell her breast.

A nurse at each hour stationed to my sleep. It is
safe / in a way / you cannot have at home

take with you. That belief / that every day /
and you must include pain.

SHHHHHHHHH, SHHHHHHH

Did I say I? For I meant *her* and *Nadja*
cracked as a European frost, blanching
the rips in her thick cotton stockings /
because she falls. You think she knows no /

others Anna, Emma, Edna, rich
men's sisters and wards / as mirror /
as moor mist broken horse its reins, really
the captain's reins in the captain's hands / a white
army headed for a red one, swarthy dispatched
in hull or coffin / how did you imagine she /

you retrieved her from a cafe just after
she crossed a Ural mountain, thru the notch
to pay with the notch, and now drinking
one of your tiny coffees on loan turning

grayer with corpse creep / Lucy or Mina
drained neatly / one of your tiny coffees
you feed her the mush of handwritten /

what are those? Poems? Love letters?
Arsenic in the pastries, tiny folds
of fat and sheen. What is beautiful /

tin back an arc like a dancer you discount
a darkened doorway / a bare room
whose is it? Like a hospital! with its thin sheet
and one stiff towel and the lock that doesn't latch.

You'll put a chair to the knob, and wipe your hand
on a handkerchief leaving / the gutter
catches it in snowy maw and there also her parcel
of letters hospital! corners a hospital! bow. Are they/

lovers' confessions. Yes you liked her dark nape
in its ahistorical plunge / intellect knew its

limited privilege

knew where / this belief that every day / pain

should've found a finer home. Without begging.
I shall never get out of this
belief every day / there are
two of us now

That pure one and I
proving neither self nor /
I'm up in a tree trying to K-I-
an orderly. What do they call them

now, big men? Click goes a nurse.
Click goes the night / watch is set
and fixed / click, never sounds the handle

I wonder, in the mammalian hospital!
Is each nipple an aperture?
You have taken me! /

to so many doctors, I cannot smell them apart.
My crotch in the crotch of an old oak tree.
Maple sugar cherry blossom apple sauce—

Who's creeping down the orchard's last alley?
That's me, this pale yellow one, with long hair
on my arms and legs, with fingers like icicles
melting drip on your tongue your hide if my breasts
are so full of jet fuel, what good does it do /

in the hospital!hospital! / to drain the poison
down / the drain / the hatch in the floor / in the
li-no center / like you would whisper a cancer /
telephone! telephone! / whisper your neighbor
a cancer / and she gets / twins.

In one version of that year everyone was brittle
worried about relevance and critical /
intervention. And in the other version flies died

in the bathtub tho it was winter / the bathtub
pinkish with iron and loose with wings or
a plague of rocks came out of /

It was twenty below. I probably agreed to be /
Nadja / my liver swelled with love, but there wasn't

for either of us / the floor was sticky.

The floor, flies, past times sticky floors,
sticky and sticking the glue babies one makes
by rubbing her hands briskly and brisker

they whisper, silk as dry skin on the sheets
bleached daily / taking pains / to bleeeee

Following a hospital! leg wound my head opened,
through the fat layer, my bone, my sleeper cell went off,
a young girl with a new cavity fevered on a gurney /

I saw her /

What was different?
I could identify the relevant vectors.
We don't / love each other / my wire mother, screw aunties,
wire veins, the wire that runs from tear duct to ear.

A vibration to keep me fluid until. I don't know
/ when. The year begins / to count again. I'm not dying

very quickly / the earth burns my tongue. I pry it apart again.
Maybe I did die. From this wound. A wire bandage

mother goes around calling my name / frostwhite
like it's hers in her mouth. I probably won't / see you again.

IN BED WITH YOUR BOOK THE NEWS THE NEWS JUST GAPES

Hand up the block. I am the chop. I am the perfect
gentleman butcher, I wrap you in slick pink paper
I wrap the block the lawyers at the judges' box I block
the box I know what kills / you went around the block
to unfather yourself you went where I went / shrug
I had a daddy he talked to me friends walked up I was never
again his daughter, I was in the future where my mother
wouldn't die she bloated my face I wasn't old, I was I was
inside someone who hated me / from the time I was inside
inside her, before, I'd been around the block, too mean
in the streets I dragged the sheets I proved all the red
all the red parts were from the knife and not the shaft.

At or near the time of birth, something blooms in me
other than those people who
                          fucked me into place, you know?
I held your hand and looked away and walked away without
my hand I looked away from it so you could know privately
how privately I loved

IMPATIENT TO BE RATIFIED A SKIN CRAWLS
ACROSS YOUR RIMS A WOUND CLOSES

Another patient whose thigh measures
the same length as mine whose hips fit discreetly
in the cradle of mine whose shoulders form the cape of mine
whose mine is depth of mine exact / and whose tomb
is locked and sealed and lost. Whose blood flows backward

whose head falls off as he rides, whose intentions release
the centaur beneath him while his hand steadies the bow.
Whose bow is my mouth neatly knit

who never saw my bow untied or my youth / my youths
centaurs passing beneath me, so often bucked did I care?

Irrelevant. Everything I shove behind the shelf
including another patient whose hand I had to look from
it bloomed in mine rare pungent fibers / bloom once,
what do I care. Bloom once and behead.

Did I think I would brave behold it? I'm vain, not foolish.

I'm dickless, I'm pond scum unreflected. What becomes
of me but an echo of you? If I were snatched
from the sky, it's more than was writ for me. All justice
is lost in the small chasm between knowing and doing.
Regret is for men. For hospital, for temperatures

for the day in your diary always marked with
its frayed wet red ribbon / as tho marking might undo.
You never gave me a thing, so why give me that?

What if instead like Christo we built an actual tin can line?
What if like a silk sheet my voice were always brushing the line,
dingier and more ragged with passage. Dingier unspun
back to the threads, back to the cocoon, until opened

the worm backed out with her brow knit and her countenance
a scar on the mulberry. What if I were a scar in your tree

and also the only leaf you could eat? That's not much
to ask / now is it / the moonrise or the sunrise or something
balefully diurnal else that wigs you back into normalcy?
Like an impoverished prophet who limped for real and so
made of the limp an extravagant gesture:

> O fuck you rose on
> my horizon brighter than
> the previous fuck

When I became alive again I couldn't help who woke / she wasn't
strong or likable. She wasn't in a cast nor sawed
free from her cast. The cast has value and its innards no mouth
so anyone who speaks from the ruin becomes a bird
who has no tongue / she substitutes a worm for her tongue.

This infectious belief.
That every day.
Must include an actual bride
and pain, her referent.

ACKNOWLEDGEMENTS

Poems from the manuscript have appeared in *Atticus Review, Bennington Review, Diode, Ghost Town Review, Interim, Jet Fuel Review, Nevertheless #ShePersisted 2*, and *Typo*.

"My Heart Through Which Her Heart Has Passed" comes from a 2001 limited translation of that name by Mark Polizzoti of Breton's previously unpublished poems.

[Oh storm-damaged sarcophagus] refers to and quotes from Elisabeth Bronfen's **The Knotted Subject**

[Having attempted and attempted again] borrows the prawns from Rosario Ferré's "The Youngest Doll."

"I come to you adorned in a moss in which barely visible organisms foment and bioluminescently suggest a foolish joy" paraphrases REM's "Near Wild Heaven."

"Shhhhhhhhh, shhhhhhhhh" borrows Sarah Vap's tiny coffees and quotes Sylvia Plath's opening line from "In Plaster," "I shall never get out of this!"

"In bed with the news and your book your book just gapes" paraphrases Amiri Baraka's poem "An Agony. As Now," "I am inside someone / who hates me."

SYSTEMS COMPOSED AND UNMADE
A CONVERSATION WITH DANIELLE PAFUNDA

Greetings! Thank you for talking to us about your process today! Can you introduce yourself, in a way that you would choose?

Hello, I'm Danielle, she/her/hers.

Why are you a poet/writer/artist?

Because I have a great deal of undelivered speech, because I believe in the capacity of poetry to articulate the previously inarticulable, because I think we each might contribute to the record of human culture, because my brain is like this, because art has the potential to meet us, activate us, create mystical and phenomenological space, because it is a place to lodge affect and aesthetic, because there is much unfair and wrong that cannot be readily corrected with logic or will alone. Because it takes some people a lifetime to learn that other humans not themselves are also sovereign, because some people never learn it. Because you can flip a weapon on its creep or light a friend's match. For vindication and revelry. And more.

I don't understand how systems of power maintain purchase. Sociopolitically, I unpack their function with feminist theories, disability studies, critical race poetics, affect theory, capitalocene critiques, but cannot convince myself of their inevitability. Systems of power dictate our relationships to other people, flora, fauna, bacteria, protists, minerals, space, time, everything. Still, these relationships have the capacity to generate phenomenological zones of resistance, ways out of power. To figure out how, I render the speculative possibilities and the violence that got us to this intersection of despair and hope.

As personal and collective trauma recklessly collude, our individual and shared cultural experience gets unmade in our hands. When experience stops making sense, poetry has the unique capacity to disrupt language's insistence on sensible expression. Where trauma resists narrative prose, the lyric articulates the inarticulable. I'm trying to find the language for what's happening to us in general, and me in particular. So, I'm not trying to produce beautiful or even necessarily good art. I'm committed, instead, to the pungency of the project, doing whatever it takes to speak a silenced ontological atmosphere, helping people name what they feel and be.

There are yet feelings we're—readers and writers, both—resistant to exploring. I often work in these minor and ugly feelings (see Cathy Park Hong, Sianne Ngai, etc), shaping the architecture of spite, shame, anxiety, silliness, irritation, impatience, indignation, and more. Like our relationships, these affects are both result of and breeding ground for oppressive conditions, and might paradoxically be our best sites of resistance. My poems, if sometimes eager to be beautiful, transcendent, uplifting, or revelatory, must also be rude, abrupt, mired, pushy, indiscreet, turgid, sharp, immature, or overbearing. I hope to insight a circuit of cringes and blooms in the reader, to shake loose from our good/bad binary. To create alternately muscular and clairvoyant lyrics.

In an ailing culture that manipulates people by insisting we become immune to our own emotional weather and our material intensities, I want to get better. I want to be re-enfranchised, less lonely, changing. I want reckoning and sanctuary in equal measure, and I want the existential ecotones only poetry provides.

When did you decide you were a poet/writer/artist (and/or: do you feel comfortable calling yourself a poet/writer/artist, what other titles or affiliations do you prefer/feel are more accurate)?

I was lucky to have many books in my childhood home and to, somehow--I imagine owing to my amped up constitution--learn to read before I started school. Writing seemed to me an organic extension of reading. Once, when I was ten, my mother, grandmother, and aunt heard me say I wanted to be a writer. "You have to be good to be a writer," they said. I knew I'd be good, in this case, but later I realized that good was not really the aspiration for me. Pungent or realized or other was the aspiration. Impossible was the aspiration.

What's a "poet" (or "writer" or "artist") anyway? What do you see as your cultural and social role (in the literary / artistic / creative community and beyond)?

The role of a poet is to articulate what previously hasn't been articulated, or articulate it somehow more effectively. Because I'm committed to social justice and sanctuary for thought and being, I have an additional charge to apply my poetry to those causes, though not necessarily in a conventionally edifying fashion. I also see my cultural role less as a creator of beauty and more as someone who sees artistic projects through to their furthest manifestations.

Talk about the process or instinct to move these poems (or your work in general) as independent entities into a body of work. How and why did this happen? Have you had this intention for a while? What encouraged and/or confounded this (or a book, in general) coming together? Was it a struggle?

This book came out of my affection for and frustration with modernism's grooms, most especially André Breton. It came out of the bad dynamic between hetero lovers in the couple-state. It came out of a consideration of Elisabeth Bronfen's *Over Her Dead Body* and the notion that masculine genius posited itself not only on feminine corpses in art and literature, but reinforced white supremacy and patriarchy by projecting a theatrically amplified whiteness, impossible standard of beauty, and biologically counterintuitive impermeability onto those corpses. It came out of chronic pain and the medical industry. It came out of the obliterating hostilities of institutions that disregard the rights of people while simultaneously co-opting those human rights for their own protection and profit. It was vexed by the limitations of my own speech, and was also encouraged by this and that infinite quality possibility.

I've used the title of Breton's *My Heart Through Which Her Heart Has Passed* (a limited edition folio of love poems) and a line or two from *Communicating Vessels*. I've reworked the narrative of *Nadja*, but not faithfully. Breton tells his protagonist's story of the love affair with Nadja and then exiles Nadja to the sanitorium. Later, in Communicating Vessels Breton recounting a dream obliquely addresses his real-life relationship to Nadja, speculating on what might happen if she, "sane or otherwise," were able to return and read his book about her. Spite asks, instead, what happens if the OG melancholy bohemian dream girl is the author and subject of her story.

Ultimately, my murky use of Breton is a way of removing the authority of men who exploit the (imagined or real) stories of women's love affairs. It refuses to grant the cis-het man's he-said copyright. I don't think readers need to be even remotely familiar with Breton to read such a common story of the exploitation a man writer insists is the necessary cost of art. He was my vehicle, but his is just one of a zillion men protagonists who use a woman unto illness or death to get where he's going or alleviate his own ennui or whatever.

For a recent visual arts take on Breton and women surrealists, read Andrea Cundy's article "Why the Resurgent Interest in Female Surrealists Needs to be Reflected in Museum Collections," which begins:

'The problem of woman,' André Breton wrote in his Second Manifeste du Surréalisme (Second Manifesto of Surrealism, 1929), 'is the most marvellous and disturbing problem in all the world.' In this short sentence, Breton laid the foundations for surrealism's infamous misogyny: women were revered and central to the movement, but as muses, not artists in their own right. Happily, in recent years, many have seen the problem in Breton's statement itself, and female surrealists are garnering much deserved late recognition. At Frieze https://frieze.com/article/why-resurgent-interest-female-surrealists-needs-be-reflected-museum-collections

What formal structures or other constrictive practices (if any) do you use in the creation of your work? Have certain teachers or instructive environments, or readings/writings/ work of other creative people informed the way you work/write?

I don't often use formal structures or constrictive practices in any conventional sense, though each book does comes with its own rules and I tend to follow them.

Worldbuilding is important to me in poetry as much as in fiction, and I need to intuit a given world's mechanics and metaphysics. Sometimes a world's rules have the quality of compulsive or magical thinking, as is true for our agreed-upon real world. Speaking of monikers, what does your title represent? How was it generated? Talk about the way you titled the book, and how your process of naming (individual pieces, sections, etc) influences you and/or colors your work specifically. Spite is an underrated ugly feeling of great value, depth, landscape, quality, etc.

What does this particular work represent to you as indicative of your method/creative practice, history, mission/intentions/hopes/plans?

This particular work is perhaps a good example of what happens to texts when I synthesize them. It charts my relationship to the work of modernists, often both compelling and vexing to me. The mission here is not necessarily a grand or noble one. This book helps me consider the risks and rewards of embodiment and particular performances of femininity, how that femininity has been historically co-opted as catalyst for the development of the masculine artist, and how it might be re-narrated (if not improved). I don't expect all art to be beautiful or even (conventionally) good. Sometimes, to succeed, a project must be flawed or even scan not-good in places. If a project is near to fully realized, then I feel it's done and ready to go out into the world.

What does this book DO (as much as what it says or contains)?

This book asks to whom the story belongs. This book takes liberties. This book speaks from a space of physical pain whose articulation is almost always assumed incomplete. This book resists and at the same time melds. This book wonders if there's positive generative possibility in those feelings or states to which we ascribe negative quality. This book exercises its grudges alongside its reverence.

What would be the best possible outcome for this book? What might it do in the world, and how will its presence as an object facilitate your creative role in your community and beyond? What are your hopes for this book, and for your practice?

I hope this book will create the harmony of vindication or recognition for some of its readers. As an object, it records elements of human experience we often think below art's notice or obstacle to art. With regard to my own practice, I hope these poems record something about how neurological firestorms informed my work during an era of acute hostility and pain. That said, I try not to indulge too many hopes for a book once it's out of my computer and head, into the reader's space. I hope, for the most part, it'll do its most self.

Let's talk a little bit about the role of poetics and creative community in social and political activism, so present in our daily lives as we face the often sobering, sometimes dangerous realities of the Capitalocene. How does your process, practice, or work otherwise interface with these conditions?

My practice always questions systems of power, and how my speakers are both composed and unmade by these systems. This book in particular considers the ways in which love can seem revolutionary and prove otherwise. In our eagerness to believe in the radical power of love, we often embrace a love that ultimately reinscribes every oppression. That's not meant to be uplifting or edifying, necessarily, but just to unpack some of the ways in which even our most intimate attachments get scripted and conscripted into the Capitalocene.

I'd be curious to hear some of your thoughts on the challenges we face in speaking and publishing across lines of race, age, ability, class, privilege, social/cultural background, gender, sexuality (and other identifiers) within the community as well as creating and maintaining safe spaces, vs. the dangers of remaining and producing in isolated "silos" and/or disciplinary and/or institutional bounds?

Systems of power reproduce themselves in any field they find purchase. Ours isn't special--plenty of breeding ground for privilege and plenty of opportunity to exploit privilege, maintain status quo. It's not just that we need to bring more voices into the mix, but that we must consciously craft spaces in which conventional hierarchies can't flourish.

ABOUT THE AUTHOR

DANIELLE PAFUNDA is the author of eight other books of prose and poetry: *The Book of Scab* (Ricochet Editions), *Beshrew* (Dusie Press), *The Dead Girls Speak in Unison* (Bloof Books), *Natural History Rape Museum* (Bloof Books), *Manhater* (Dusie Press), *Iatrogenic* (Noemi Press), *My Zorba* (Bloof Books), and *Pretty Young Thing* (Soft Skull Press). She's published two chapbooks: *Cram* (Essay Press) and *When You Left Me in the Rutted Terrain of Our Love at the Border, Which I Could Not Cross, Remaining a Citizen of This Corrupt Land* (Birds of Lace). Her work has appeared in three editions of *Best American Poetry*, *BAX: Best American Experimental Writing*, the Academy of American Poets Poem-a-Day, and a number of anthologies and journals. She teaches at Rochester Institute of Technology.

WHY PRINT / DOCUMENT?

The Operating System uses the language "print document" to differentiate from the book-object as part of our mission to distinguish the act of documentation-in-book-FORM from the act of publishing as a backwards-facing replication of the book's agentive *role* as it may have appeared the last several centuries of its history. Ultimately, I approach the book as TECHNOLOGY: one of a variety of printed documents (in this case, bound) that humans have invented and in turn used to archive and disseminate ideas, beliefs, stories, and other evidence of production.

Ownership and use of printing presses and access to (or restriction of printed materials) has long been a site of struggle, related in many ways to revolutionary activity and the fight for civil rights and free speech all over the world. While (in many countries) the contemporary quotidian landscape has indeed drastically shifted in its access to platforms for sharing information and in the widespread ability to "publish" digitally, even with extremely limited resources, the importance of publication on physical media has not diminished. In fact, this may be the most critical time in recent history for activist groups, artists, and others to insist upon learning, establishing, and encouraging personal and community documentation practices. Hear me out.

With The OS's print endeavors I wanted to open up a conversation about this: the ultimately radical, transgressive act of creating PRINT /DOCUMENTATION in the digital age. It's a question of the archive, and of history: who gets to tell the story, and what evidence of our life, our behaviors, our experiences are we leaving behind? We can know little to nothing about the future into which we're leaving an unprecedentedly digital document trail — but we can be assured that publications, government agencies, museums, schools, and other institutional powers that be will continue to leave BOTH a digital and print version of their production for the official record. Will we?

As a (rogue) anthropologist and long time academic, I can easily pull up many accounts about how lives, behaviors, experiences — how THE STORY of a time or place — was pieced together using the deep study of correspondence, notebooks, and other physical documents which are no longer the norm in many lives and practices. As we move our creative behaviors towards digital note taking, and even audio and video, what can we predict about future technology that is in any way assuring that our stories will be accurately told – or told at all? How will we leave these things for the record?

In these documents we say:
WE WERE HERE, WE EXISTED, WE HAVE A DIFFERENT STORY

- Elæ [Lynne DeSilva-Johnson], Founder/Creative Director
THE OPERATING SYSTEM, Brooklyn NY 2018

RECENT & FORTHCOMING
OS PRINT::DOCUMENTS and PROJECTS, 2019-20

2020

Institution is a Verb: A Panoply Performance Lab Compilation
Poetry Machines: Letters for a Near Future - Margaret Rhee
My Phone Lies to me: Fake News Poetry Workshops as
Radical Digital Media Literacy - Alexandra Juhasz, Ed.
Goodbye Wolf-Nik DeDominic
Spite - Danielle Pafunda
Acid Western - Robert Balun
Cupping - Joseph Han

KIN(D)* TEXTS AND PROJECTS

Hoax - Joey De Jesus
#Survivor - Joanna C. Valente
Intergalactic Travels: Poems from a Fugutive Alien - Alan Pelaez Lopez
RoseSunWater - Angel Dominguez

GLOSSARIUM: UNSILENCED TEXTS AND TRANSLATIONS

Zugunruhe - Kelly Martinez Grandal (tr. Margaret Randall)
En el entre / In the between: Selected Antena Writings -
Antena Aire (Jen Hofer & John Pluecker)
Black and Blue Partition ('Mistry) - Monchoachi (tr. Patricia Hartland)
Si la musique doit mourir (If music were to die) -
Tahar Bekri (tr. Amira Rammah)
Farvernes Metafysik: Kosmisk Farvelære (The Metaphysics of Color: A Cosmic Theory of Color) - Ole Jensen Nyrén (tr. Careen Shannon)
Híkurí (Peyote) - José Vincente Anaya (tr. Joshua Pollock)

2019

Ark Hive-Marthe Reed
I Made for You a New Machine and All it Does is Hope - Richard Lucyshyn
Illusory Borders-Heidi Reszies
A Year of Misreading the Wildcats - Orchid Tierney
Of Color: Poets' Ways of Making | An Anthology of Essays on Transformative Poetics - Amanda Galvan Huynh & Luisa A. Igloria, Editors

KIN(D)* TEXTS AND PROJECTS

A Bony Framework for the Tangible Universe-D. Allen
Opera on TV-James Brunton
Hall of Waters-Berry Grass
Transitional Object-Adrian Silbernagel

GLOSSARIUM: UNSILENCED TEXTS AND TRANSLATIONS

Śnienie / Dreaming - Marta Zelwan/Krystyna Sakowicz, (Poland, trans. Victoria Miluch)
High Tide Of The Eyes - Bijan Elahi (Farsi-English/dual-language) trans. Rebecca Ruth Gould and Kayvan Tahmasebian
In the Drying Shed of Souls: Poetry from Cuba's Generation Zero Katherine Hedeen and Víctor Rodríguez Núñez, translators/editors
Street Gloss - Brent Armendinger with translations of Alejandro Méndez, Mercedes Roffé, Fabián Casas, Diana Bellessi, and Néstor Perlongher (Argentina)
Operation on a Malignant Body - Sergio Loo (Mexico, trans. Will Stockton)
Are There Copper Pipes in Heaven - Katrin Ottarsdóttir (Faroe Islands, trans. Matthew Landrum)

---

for our full catalog please visit:
https://squareup.com/store/the-operating-system/

deeply discounted Book of the Month and Chapbook Series subscriptions are a great way to support the OS's projects and publications!
sign up at: http://www.theoperatingsystem.org/subscribe-join/

DOC U MENT
/däkyəmənt/

First meant "instruction" or "evidence," whether written or not.

noun - a piece of written, printed, or electronic matter that provides information or evidence or that serves as an official record
verb - record (something) in written, photographic, or other form
synonyms - paper - deed - record - writing - act - instrument

[*Middle English, precept, from Old French, from Latin documentum, example, proof, from docre, to teach; see dek- in Indo-European roots.*]

Who is responsible for the manufacture of value?

Based on what supercilious ontology have we landed in a space where we vie against other creative people in vain pursuit of the fleeting credibilities of the scarcity economy, rather than freely collaborating and sharing openly with each other in ecstatic celebration of MAKING?

While we understand and acknowledge the economic pressures and fear-mongering that threatens to dominate and crush the creative impulse, we also believe that **now more than ever we have the tools to relinquish agency via cooperative means,** fueled by the fires of the Open Source Movement.

Looking out across the invisible vistas of that rhizomatic parallel country we can begin to see our community beyond constraints, in the place where intention meets resilient, proactive, collaborative organization.

Here is a document born of that belief, sown purely of imagination and will. When we document we assert. We print to make real, to reify our being there. When we do so with mindful intention to address our process, to open our work to others, to create beauty in words in space, to respect and acknowledge the strength of the page we now hold physical, a thing in our hand, we remind ourselves that, like Dorothy: *we had the power all along, my dears.*

THE PRINT! DOCUMENT SERIES
is a project of
the trouble with bartleby
in collaboration with
the operating system

www.ingramcontent.com/pod-product-compliance
Lightning Source LLC
Chambersburg PA
CBHW030347100526
44592CB00010B/861